'Get into'
Carpentry

'Get into'
Carpentry
with Roy Day

This edition produced exclusively for

WHSMITH

ABOUT THE AUTHOR

Trained as an interior designer, Roy Day has spent many years as a writer, broadcaster and television presenter on the various aspects of home improvement. More recently he has diversified into landscape design and produced his first documentary for BBC television. 'A Garden for Chelsea' was based on his own award-winning garden at the Chelsea Flower Show. Roy Day is currently dividing his time between writing the new series of 'Get Into' books and producing more programmes on home interest and arts subjects for video and television. The first four titles in this new mini-book series are *Get into Decorating*, *Get into Carpentry*, *Get into Plumbing* and *Get into Home Electrics*.

Cover photography by Michael Plomer

**This edition produced exclusively for
W H Smith**

Published by
Deans International Publishing
52–54 Southwark Street, London SE1 1UA
A division of The Hamlyn Publishing Group Limited
London · New York · Sydney · Toronto

Copyright © The Hamlyn Publishing Group Limited 1983
ISBN 0 603 03113 7

Printed in Italy

Contents

ACKNOWLEDGMENTS

The author would like to thank the following for their co-operation in providing photographs: Neill Tools Ltd; Stanley Tools; Black & Decker; GKN; Allied Steel and Wire Ltd., Copydex Ltd.

Some of the illustrations in this book have been published previously by The Hamlyn Publishing Group Limited under the title *House Repair and Home Maintenance*.

Introduction

Not so long ago the word carpentry would have conjured up the image of dovetail joints, a stout workbench covered with tools and a workshop floor strewn with wood shavings. This was the image of the skilled craftsman whose knowledge of tools, techniques and timber stretched far beyond the realms of ordinary mortals.

This has completely changed with the do-it-yourself revolution. Sooner or later enthusiasm for home improvement dictates that we take up the hammer and chisel. It may be the necessity of putting up a simple shelf that makes us take the first step, or a door which has suddenly become difficult to close. Whatever the reason, we will be involved with carpentry for the very first time and be faced with problems which will have to be overcome if the finished job is to be deemed successful.

In this book we look at the range of materials which can be used, consider what is needed to make up a comprehensive tool kit as well as explaining the various techniques which are employed when doing basic carpentry.

A bewildering range of tools faces the first-time buyer and money can be spent on a purchase which will only be put to good use once. Costly mistakes like this should be avoided. There is great satisfaction to be derived from doing even the simplest job in the home well and it is hoped that the following pages will help you to get into carpentry and derive much pleasure as a result.

If you are to take carpentry seriously you will need to build up a collection of tools, learn to use them correctly and above all keep them in good working order.

A good basic range of handtools are all you need to tackle most of the jobs which are likely to crop up around the house. You will find that some of these tools you will use time and time again, and it is for this reason that choosing a quality article from the start pays dividends in the long run.

Complete your first job successfully with simple basic tools and the chances are that you will soon progress to more ambitious work, tackling those things which you had previously considered beyond your skill and expertise. It is at this stage that you will benefit from knowing what materials are available to work with.

Materials

NATURAL TIMBER

Softwood is now officially sized in metric measurements, for example 50mm × 25mm/2in × 1in. Old habits die hard and a lot of timber is still ordered in traditional imperial sizes by both amateur and tradesman alike. The merchant will meet your requirements for any cut sizes but the pricing will be based on metre length costs.

Unfortunately the quality of softwood can vary a great deal and all too often very poor quality timber is passed off onto the unsuspecting amateur. As a general rule, softwood is produced from the evergreen conifer family of trees. A great deal of this is imported into the country from the coniferous regions of the world and it is received by the importers in a variety of grades. When you go to select softwood there are one or two points to look for, before purchasing the lengths that you need.

First look across the sawn end of the timber. If the rings run the shortest way across the thickness of the timber, it has been quarter cut from the log and will be less likely to warp. If on the other hand the rings run the longest way along the length of the saw cut, then the plank has been flat sawn from the log. Knots can cause problems in a piece of wood. If they are actively resinous, then that piece of wood should not be used as decorative facing timber. Always scrape away any resin and coat the surface with shellac knotting before priming it for painting.

Steer clear of wood where the knots are dead and coming loose, this is the sign of weakness in the structure of the timber. Another sign of weakness is splitting which is usually due to the timber being allowed to dry out too rapidly.

Sometimes you will find a plank with bark along one edge, this is known as waney edged and should be avoided. It will have a discoloured band of sapwood inside the bark which is prone to decay and attack by insects. Finally look out for signs of grey staining in softwood, it is usually caused by exposure to sea water during the voyage and remains permanently to discolour the wood.

Planed or finished timber is slightly more expensive than rough sawn wood and although the metric sizes are listed as the same for both, the actual dimensions of the width and thickness of planed timber will be about 5mm less than its sawn counterpart. Bear this in mind when measuring up and calculating the timber sizes that you need. Look along the length of each plank to see that it is as straight as possible before purchasing. Badly warped lengths are usually the result of poor seasoning and can present you with problems when you come to use it.

A word here about the seasoning of timber. Kiln-dried timber is a quick, controlled method of reducing the moisture content in newly felled trees after they have been cut up in the saw mills. Air drying is another method of seasoning, where the moisture content is reduced over a longer period.

If seasoned wood is left in a damp atmosphere, it will soak up moisture and swell. For this reason you should leave it in a room for a week or two before working with it. It will then settle to equal the moisture level of its surroundings and remain more stable when it is finally worked. This is particularly important where central heating is fitted as it can have a rapid drying effect on timber. By contrast an exposed outer door can swell in damp weather.

Here the author shows how timber cladding, laminate, mirror tiles and veneer-faced boards can be used together for attractive wall units.

HARDWOODS

Solid hardwood is extremely expensive and it is unlikely that you would use this unless it was required for a hard-wearing surface, such as a doorstep or as a decorative timber for a mantle shelf.

A good piece of hardwood can be sliced and used as lippings and edgings to shelves, doors and drawer fronts. In this way it can be put to very economic use.

Look out for secondhand pieces from furniture or old houses. Demolition contractors often pro-

vide a good supply source and as long as it is free of
infestation, hardwood will store well until you find
a use for it.

MAN-MADE BOARDS

Man-made board is largely produced from natural
timber in chip or veneer form, held together with a
high proportion of glue. A range of sizes is
available including large sheets, the most common
being 2440mm × 1220mm/8ft × 4ft.

Some of these can be used outside but most
absorb moisture rapidly which restricts their use to

inside the home. The main advantage to working with man-made board is that it tends to be cheaper than natural timber, to conform to a regular production standard and to be less likely to warp. However, the glue content tends to blunt sharp tools quickly.

Chipboard

Chipboard is made by bonding together wood shavings with a synthetic resin under heat and pressure. Quality varies from a coarse surface board made from large single particles throughout, to the more common smooth-surfaced chipboards where finer particles are used on the outer faces. Other grades include flame-retardent boards suitable for roofing under felt and heavy duty flooring with tongued and grooved edges.

Chipboard requires very careful preparation if it is to be painted. The surface is porous and will need priming with a special chipboard primer. A certain amount of surface filling must be done to provide a really smooth surface for the finishing coats. It is not recommended where there is any likelihood of condensation affecting it, such as on window sills and close to washing areas in kitchens and bathrooms. Once moisture penetrates the board it deteriorates rapidly with the development of mildew and rot.

Chipboard should really be covered by impervious material which makes it ideally suited for work surfaces which are finished with laminated plastic or ceramic tiling. Even under these conditions all edges which might be vulnerable to moisture should be thoroughly sealed. There are several thicknesses of chipboard available but 12mm/$\frac{1}{2}$in and 18mm/$\frac{3}{4}$in are the two most commonly used.

Plastic-faced and wood-veneered chipboard is used frequently in the furniture industry. It is also used for free standing and built-in units in the home. Care has to be taken to ensure that the decorative surface of this type of board is not damaged while working with it.

Hardboard

Hardboard is made from softwood pulp and is a thinner material than chipboard although thick grades are available. As it is flexible, it can be bent around fairly tight curves but it does need an adequate number of fixing battens to hold it rigidly in place.

Standard hardboard is frequently used in the home for pelmets, facing doors and making toys. It has a smooth surface one side and a textured surface on the other. Most stockists carry large panels, the most common size being 2440mm × 1220mm/8ft × 4ft as well as a range of smaller cut sizes.

As a safeguard against hardboard buckling, it is recommended that sheets should be seasoned before use. This is done by scrubbing the back of each large sheet with one litre of water, then laying the sheets back to back for two or three days in the room before using them.

Tempered hardboard is treated with oil and is more water resistant, this can be used outside for fascia panels. There are also hardboards which are smooth on both sides, some with attractive perforated patterns, as well as the pegboard type which is ideal for display purposes.

Plywood

Plywood is made of thin veneers of wood which are glued together. It always consists of an odd number of sheets with the grain running in alternate directions to give stability. This means that the grain of the two outside layers will always run in the same direction. Apart from being graded by the ply thickness, for example 3-ply, 5-ply or multi-ply, its classification depends upon whether soft or hardwood has been used in its construction and the type of adhesive used to bond it together.

For any outside work use a good resin-bonded plywood with a WPB marking. This type of exterior grade is also ideal for use inside where moisture is likely to be present. A standard interior plywood will break down and curl at the edges if subjected to damp conditions and should only be used for construction in dry places.

Thicknesses range from 3–24mm/$\frac{1}{8}$in–1in, and the thinnest grades can be curved successfully. A good quality 18mm/$\frac{3}{4}$in plywood is a strong warp-free material to work with but is expensive.

Blockboard

This is a cheaper material than plywood and should be considered as a more economic substitute for building fitted wardrobes and any other internal structures.

Blockboard consists of lengths of softwood laid side by side between two layers of birchwood veneer with the grain running in the opposite direction, this gives greater stability along the length of the board. The softwood strips can be loose or missing in places which means that the sawn ends across ·the width of the board will require lipping if they are exposed to view.

Here the author has designed and built a shelf display which is carried by a Tebrax system of aluminium supports. The shelves have been formed from white plastic-faced chipboard with the sawn edges lipped with narrow strips of mahogany. The same materials have been used to make the fascias and ceiling panels. To give a greater sense of space, mirror tiles have been taken down to the floor on the adjacent wall.

A small recess in a room lends itself to this style of treatment, where mirror tiles can be placed behind the shelving to create an illusion of depth. It illustrates how off-cuts from man-made boards can

be used where space is limited to create an attractive focal point. The hardwood lippings were cut from secondhand rough-sawn mahogany rails and planed down to the thickness of the board before fixing.

If you have enough storage space available in a loft, shed or garage, avoid the temptation to throw away off-cuts of any materials you use. There will always be a use for odd pieces at some stage in the future. It might be just a small length that you need for shuttering, if you are about to concrete the edge of a step for example – here the quality of the timber would not be important. Even the smallest slivers of discarded material can be used for packing wedges behind wall battens, and it is then that you will be pleased that you held on to all the bits and pieces.

Sometimes you will even find that you can glue small sections together of various sizes to make up a workpiece for something. Plywood and chipboard can be assembled in this way and then covered in laminated plastic to provide a shelf of a specific thickness.

It is useful to have a place to work in the home but if space is limited and you are without any workshop facilities all is not lost. Many of the jobs will be undertaken in the room where the carpentry is required, and if all the preparatory work cannot be done there, it is often possible to improvise a work space in the smallest of back yards.

Your greatest asset will be the tools that you use, having them readily accessible and in good working order when you need them. Good tools are expensive and the cost can be prohibitive when you come to consider doing a job and have to purchase one or more items to carry it out in addition to the materials required. If you are starting from scratch, then build up your tool kit slowly, but as you accumulate more tools keep them together in one place, preferably where it is dry. Nothing can be more annoying than to have to search the house for specific tools which are scattered far and wide.

So let us consider some of the more essential carpentry tools, including power tools and explain how to use and maintain them.

Saws

A professional carpenter will have at least three different types of handsaw for cutting natural timber. A rip saw for cutting along the grain, a cross cut saw for cutting across the grain and a tenon saw for making fine precision saw cuts both along and across the grain. Each one of these is available in different sizes and you should take the size which feels most comfortable to hold and use – the balance should feel right in the hand.

Now consider the teeth. There will be a certain number of these every 25mm/1in and the blade will be marked accordingly. For example 5 teeth will be shown as 6 points, 14 teeth as 15 points and so on. The more teeth there are, the finer the cut will be and a fine cutting saw is always recommended for hardwood which is why a tenon saw is used on fine cabinet work.

The teeth will be formed a certain way. For rip sawing they will have flat chisel edges for running along the grain fibres and the cutting action with this saw is always on the forward down stroke. Most rip saws have either 4- or 5-point blades. The teeth on a cross cut saw have sharp points for scoring across the grain fibres and tenon saw teeth are sharpened in a similar manner.

Along every saw blade alternate teeth are bent slightly in opposite directions – this is known as the set of the saw and provides a sufficient width of cut to allow the saw blade to pass through it easily.

A good universal panel saw will do most things

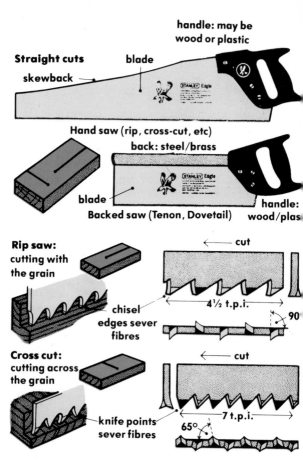

Straight cuts

skewback

blade

handle: may be
wood or plastic

Hand saw (rip, cross-cut, etc)

back: steel/brass

blade

Backed saw (Tenon, Dovetail)

handle:
wood/plas

Rip saw:
cutting with
the grain

chisel
edges sever
fibres

← cut

4½ t.p.i.

90°

Cross cut:
cutting across
the grain

knife points
sever fibres

← cut

7 t.p.i.

65°

that are required by the handyman and a 550mm/22in 8 point is a good average size blade.

Let us see what is the best way of using a panel saw. The grip on the saw handle is important. Your hand will follow the contour of its shape with the index finger pointing straight along the side of the blade. The workpiece should be placed on a trestle or other low firm support and held steady with your knee unless you have a vice to hold it securely.

Remember to cut on the waste side of your

marked line, as at least 1.5mm/$\frac{1}{16}$in will be lost in the cut. To start the cut, place your free thumb close to the line and gently draw the saw back against the side of it. This will mark a slight groove in the timber without any risk of cutting your thumb. NEVER push the saw forward with your thumb in close proximity, as this is extremely dangerous. Just watch a carpenter and see how the guide groove is formed on the back stroke.

Once the saw is ready to move forward in the groove, place your free hand wide and forward of the cutting position, ultimately using it to support the waste section before the final cutting stroke is made – this will prevent any tearing away at the edges. It helps to hold the saw at a steep angle of about 60° when ripping along the grain and at a shallower one of about 45° when cross cutting.

Cutting through timber squarely is usually the most difficult thing to accomplish as a beginner. Practice is the only answer, so try a few trial cuts on some scrap wood. Note which way you tend to tilt the saw by looking at the completed saw cut. You will find that this is a natural angle which you will keep repeating unless you make a conscious effort to correct it by pulling the blade in the opposite direction while you saw. After a while you will be amazed how well you can follow a marked line squarely through the timber. It may help you to clamp another straight length of timber against the cutting line and saw against it – it will prevent the saw from wandering. Incidentally, Teflon coated blades are less likely to jam and they also offer added protection against rust.

If a saw is kept really sharp, far less effort is required to use it. Unfortunately it is the cutting up of man-made boards, especially chipboard which quickly takes the cutting edge off a good saw blade. This is due to the high density of resin in the board.

The hardpoint saw has the special hardened teeth which will keep sharp for up to five times as

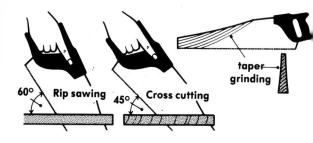

60° **Rip sawing** 45° **Cross cutting** **taper grinding**

long as the conventional saw. When they do finally begin to lose their edge, the teeth cannot be filed in the normal way but they can be sharpened by using a fine-grained whet stone. Simply lay the saw flat on the table then run the whet stone twice along the full run of the teeth from the tip towards the handle. Then turn the blade over and repeat the process. When the teeth on a hardpoint saw get beyond sharpening they can be guillotined off and new teeth can be cut as a conventional saw.

A general-purpose hardpoint panel saw should meet your requirements for cutting most boards and lengths of natural timber, but if you intend to progress to fine cabinet work then you will need a tenon saw.

This fine-toothed saw has a rigid spine along its back and should be used in a flat position with the entire length of the blade in contact with the workpiece. A 15-point 250mm/10in tenon saw is ideal for most precision jobs working with both hardwood and softwood.

If you plan to fine-cut a lot of tougher materials such as laminated plastic, then it would be advisable to get a small veneer saw without a spine but with hardpoint teeth. This will save the wear and tear on your tenon saw. This type of veneer saw will cut through thin ply easily as well as being useful as a floorboard saw. The hardpoint teeth extend along the round edge at the back of the blade for cutting slots or grooves through the middle of a surface.

When you have finished using a saw, put it back in its protective sleeve and hang it vertically to keep the blade from bending.

Any good quality saw will last indefinitely if it is kept in good working order, and this means being sharpened as soon as the teeth begin to lose their cutting edge. You can either attempt this yourself or take the saw to a shop which offers a sharpening service.

Sharpening a saw is a skilled job but certainly not one beyond the scope of the patient amateur. It entails two different operations, both calling for the saw blade to be held firmly in a vice. A file is used to sharpen each individual tooth to the correct angle and depth which will vary depending on whether the blade is to be used for ripping or cross cutting. A special tool is available for this operation and it can

How to hold

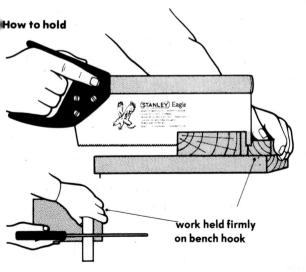

work held firmly on bench hook

25

be adjusted to accommodate any type of handsaw. When the sharpening process is complete the teeth have to be set to provide the width of cut in the timber for the blade to move through. Another special tool is available to set these teeth to the correct angle. It is known as a saw set tool and has an adjustable anvil which is controlled by a screw.

Although this is a job which you might not want to tackle until you have gained more experience in working with carpentry tools, it is important to know that specialist tools are available to make the job easier. It becomes increasingly difficult to find good local saw-sharpening agents and in the long term it may be necessary for more saw owners to carry out this type of service themselves.

All of the saws which have been covered so far are limited to cutting straight lines in any direction across timber or boards. From time to time you may need to cut curves or even large apertures from workpieces and for this you will require a different type of saw. Sawing curves can present a problem when you are faced with the task for the first time, so let us consider alternative tools which are available to tackle the job.

Coping saw

This is useful for cutting curved edges which should be less than 12mm/$\frac{1}{2}$in thick. After drilling a pilot hole, pass the thin blade through it and fit the ends into the coping saw frame and tighten – the blade should be rigid but not over taut. The only limitation with this type of saw is that it will only cut as far into the timber as the distance between the blade and the saw frame.

Bow saw

This is the larger version of the coping saw used more by specialists. It has a timber frame and is suitable for cutting curves in timber and boards thicker than 12mm/$\frac{1}{2}$in.

Pad or keyhole saw

The pad saw can be used where the limitations of the frame size of a coping saw or bow saw restrict the cutting of an opening well inside the edges of a panel. The narrow blade is clamped into the pad handle and then used by passing it through a pilot hole drilled through the material to be cut. This is a useful tool which can utilize broken hacksaw blades for cutting purposes.

Hacksaws

Although both the large and junior hacksaw are used primarily for metalwork, it is worthwhile keeping the inexpensive junior hacksaw as part of your carpenter's tool kit. There may be occasions when you need to cut through old nails or screws during the course of working with old timber, and with a hacksaw blade you will be well equipped to deal with the problem. It is as well to realize that there are a whole range of different types of blade to fit the large hacksaw frame and if you intend to extend your activities into metalwork, it is worth familiarizing yourself with these.

Tree-pruning saw

Always resist the temptation to take a good carpentry saw to the job of tree pruning, as it is the quickest way to ruin it. If you have a lot of this type of work to do in your garden, then it is far better to acquire a tree-pruning saw which is designed specifically for dealing with green timber without excessive hard work.

ELECTRIC SAWS

Second only to the electric drill, an electric jigsaw is the most useful power tool to have in your kit. Available either as an attachment to a power drill or as independent unit, the jigsaw will carry out many of the tasks which handsaws are frequently used for.

The one great advantage of using this type of power saw is that replaceable blades are cheap and a complete range are available for cutting different materials. This is well worth bearing in mind if you plan to saw a considerable amount of chipboard. You will find that perfectly straight saw cuts can be achieved by using a timber straight edge as a guide, or working with the fence attachment. Similarly, pockets can be cut accurately from the centre of boards with a minimum of effort.

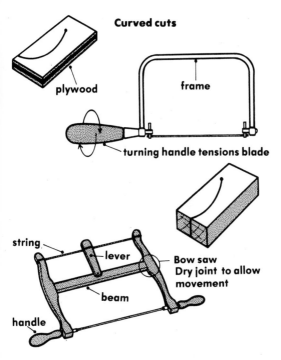

Curved cuts

plywood

frame

turning handle tensions blade

string

lever

Bow saw
Dry joint to allow
movement

beam

handle

*Most of the saws which are suitable for cutting
shapes have one thing in common, the blades are
easily replaceable. They tend to be on the thin side
and fragile, consequently have a tendency to break
if mishandled. Use them correctly and they will last
a long time. Compared with the cost a good
handsaw blade, replaceable blades are inexpensive
and this is an important consideration to bear in
mind when purchasing.*

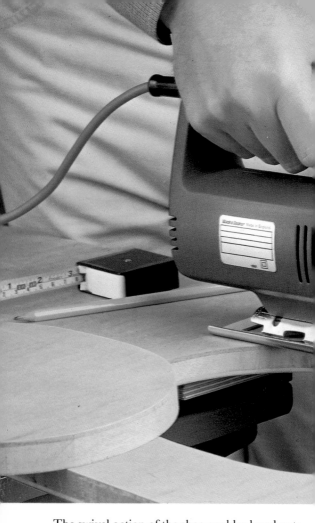

The swivel action of the shoe enables bevel cuts to be run the entire length of the work. When cutting veneers or fine laminates a clean edge can be formed by clamping the material tightly between off-cuts of plywood. Take care to follow the accepted safety code when working with the power saw. Only make adjustments to the unit and blade changes, with the power supply switched off.

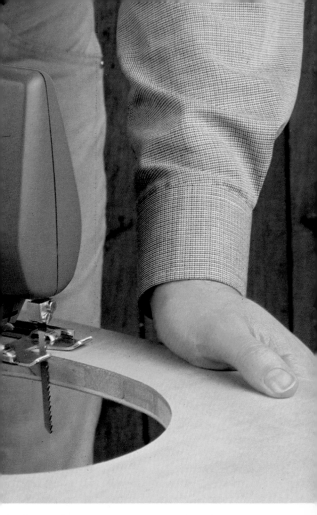

Lay the saw on its side when not in use and lock it out of reach of children when you have finished using it. Circular saws and band saws are available to the home carpenter. These units are useful if you intend to set up a saw bench in your workshop to cut timber regularly but compared with the versatility of the jigsaw unit, these other saws are for more specialized jobs.

Workbenches

Where space allows, the keen woodworker will manage to install a proper workbench complete with built-in vice – this is usually to be found in a convenient corner of the garage with a window ideally place above it. The more fortunate may even have the facilities of a spare room in an attic or basement at their disposal – a luxury indeed in an era when space is at a premium.

Unfortunately the beginner frequently has to resort to an old chair or stool for a saw horse, with the kitchen table serving as a base for all the remaining activities. Certainly there are a great number of people who manage to work perfectly well within these limitations, and who will doubt-less continue to do so for the foreseeable future. However a good workbench is desirable and does make life easier, and if it is also portable then the advantages are great indeed.

A considerable range of fixed benches are on the market for permanent siting in a workshop and the finish of some at the top end of the range is so beautiful that it almost seems a crime to work on them. But these are very much for the professional craftsman or the very dedicated, affluent amateur.

The development of the Workmate bench has certainly solved the dual problem of limited space and portability and has now become the most valuable acquisition in the home workshop. Its compact folding design allows easy transportation from place to place as well as overcoming the problem of storage or permanent siting.

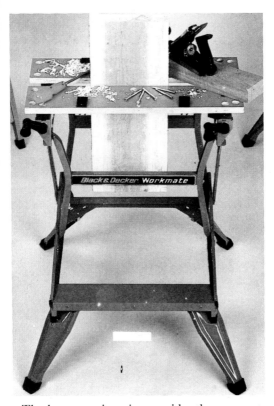

The long tapering vice provides the answer to many gripping problems, not only where woodwork is concerned but also for plumbing and car-maintenance repair work to mention just two other activities where it can be employed to advantage. The long vice will also act as clamp for certain gluing operations.

When investing in a Workmate bench, look at the various options which are open. After careful consideration you might consider that it would pay to go for the dual-height model. This will provide a comfortable working position for sawing and allow certain jobs to be done sitting on the bench.

Drills

Choosing an electric drill can be a bewildering task for the first-time buyer, but there are a few guidelines for looking at the wide variety that are available on the market today.

If you consider the various uses to which it might be put, you will soon realize that one of the prime requirements of a power drill is robustness. Although a light-weight unit will suffice for drilling the occasional hole in timber, metal and brickwork, the motor could burn out rather quickly if it is subjected to a demanding workload.

Decide whether you want to use attachments with the drill and if so will the unit which you have in mind be strong enough to power them over long periods. Wherever possible purchase more power units than are needed. It is often the case that when your enthusiasm for carpentry and other do-it-yourself pursuits takes hold, you will want to keep your drill to hand purely for drilling operations and it is at this stage that fixing attachments to it becomes a chore. You may even regret purchasing the attachment and feel that the money would have been better spent on a separate unit. Keep this in mind from the start and do not rush into buying too much equipment – remember that it has got to serve for a considerable time.

Variable speed is an essential facility which can be provided by a two-speed selecter, but there is a lot to be said for trigger control where the revolutions can be built up from zero to maximum

speed by exerting gentle pressure with the finger. Very slow initial speed is helpful when drilling into highly polished surfaces such as ceramic tile. Slow speed can also help to keep dust to a minimum because often it is the speed of the motor which causes dust to be dispersed freely into the atmosphere, instead of dropping from the mouth of the hole to be collected in an open plastic bag fixed immediately below the drill position. There are two other features which should be incorporated into the drill if it is to give a good and lasting all-round service.

35

The first is a hammer action also known as a percussion drill. This facility helps considerably when drilling into dense masonry and concrete. The vibration on the drill tip at slow speed helps to smash the stones and coarse aggregate in the concrete making the drilling operation that much easier to undertake.

The other important requirement is a 13mm/$\frac{1}{2}$in chuck to take the maximum size drill bits. There is a considerable advantage to be gained if you have the capability of drilling through a solid outside wall from one side only.

Some electric drills have an overload cut-out built into their circuitry. This will automatically prevent the motor from burning out if it is worked too hard for long periods. If this safeguard is not incorporated into your drill then take extra care when you undertake heavy jobs with the unit. Switch off at the first sign of the body of the drill getting warm and allow it to cool thoroughly before using it again.

Most drills are self lubricating and need little in the way of servicing if they are cared for and kept free of dust building up in the ventilation outlets around the body.

Hand drills

A small hand drill has a chuck capacity of about 8mm/$\frac{1}{16}$in so it is capable of boring relatively small holes and you may find that it is an unnecessary acquisition once you have an electric drill. The one great advantage of a hand drill is that it can be used in situations where electric power is unobtainable.

Hand brace

This is very much a professional carpenter's tool but is not used to the same extent by the home handyman. It will take a large range of auger bits for boring holes through thick pieces of timber such as rafters and timber joists. The ratchet action

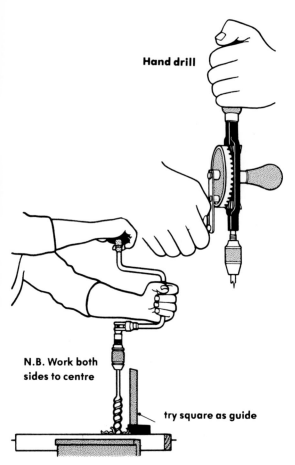

Hand drill

N.B. Work both sides to centre

try square as guide

enables the boring to be done in confined spaces where a complete turn of the brace handle is not possible. Auger bits will remain sharp as they are confined to working mainly with softwood. Twist drills on the other hand can lose their cutting edge fairly rapidly depending on the work they have done.

When using a hand drill or brace, try to keep the twist drill or auger bit in a vertical line at right angles to the workpiece.

Masonry drills have to be sent away for sharpening once the cutting edge has gone but it is possible to keep twist drills sharp yourself. You will need a special sharpening tool to do it.

The drill is clamped into the sharpener and wheeled across a piece of abrasive paper. When one side of the drill tip has been sharpened, the drill is turned 180° and the process is repeated. One of the problems experienced in sharpening a twist drill satisfactorily is to keep the tip balanced to a perfect central point. This is almost impossible to do accurately by hand which makes the sharpening tool a valuable asset for keeping your drills permanently in good cutting order.

Planes and Chisels

No carpentry enthusiast would be without a smoothing plane for skimming down timber to the required finished dimensions but it is a tool which the beginner could well manage without, particularly where pre-finished material is used. The same, however, cannot be said about a small block plane. Whereas a smoothing plane is around 245mm/9¾in long and requires two hands to operate it, a handy size block plane is about 150mm/6in long and can be comfortably held with one hand. It is a versatile little tool which can be used for skimming and smoothing uneven timber although naturally not with the same degree of precision as the longer bench planes.

Fitted with an adjustable mouth this small low-angle plane will effectively trim the end grain of timber and the sawn edges of veneered boards, as well as slicing fine slivers from the edge of plastic laminate. To do this efficiently close the mouth right down, set the blade fine and work towards the centre from each edge in turn.

All plane blades must be kept razor sharp and unfortunately chipboard core boards tend to blunt a blade rather quickly in the same way that saw teeth lose their cutting edge due to the high resin content of the material.

The inexperienced may not realize that, like a new chisel, a new plane is supplied with a blade which is not sharp and ready for use. It will require honing on an oil-stone to provide a fine cutting edge before you start to work with it.

If you look closely at a new blade you will see that a shallow angle of 25° has been ground at the cutting edge and that a coat of clear lacquer has been applied for protection by the manufacturer.

This lacquer will be removed when a second steeper angle of 30° is formed at the edge of the existing ground angle. For this crucial honing process you will require an oil-stone and some thin lubricating oil. A good oil-stone will last you for many years if it is looked after and kept in a wooden box. A fine-surface stone is required for successful honing and it is advisable to get a combination stone which has a fine surface on one side and a coarser surface on the reverse.

Two lengths of stone are commonly available, one is 150mm/6in but the longer one 200mm/8in is preferable as you can spread the wear more evenly during the process of sharpening your blades. The first stage of honing is comparatively simple. After applying a few drops of oil to the smooth surface, lay the flat underside of the blade directly onto the stone, and applying pressure with the fingers, slide the blade backwards and forwards a few times. When you lift the blade and wipe away the oil, a mirror polish will have been formed directly under the bevel edge. In the process of polishing the underside you will have rubbed out the fine scratches which are formed during the manufacture of the steel.

The next stage is very difficult and should be carried out with the help of a honing guide, unless you have considerable experience of using a stone. A honing guide will hold the blade steady at the correct angle to form the secondary honing edge. Lubricate the stone with a few drops of oil and then roll the guide in a figure of eight pattern along the entire length of the stone a few times. When the oil is wiped away you will find that a very fine wire burr has been formed along the cutting edge. This burr is usually wiped away with the oil from the blade; if you see it on the cloth it is an indication that the correct degree of sharpness has been achieved.

The art of honing a blade without the help of a honing guide, is the art of holding the blade at a constant angle throughout the movement backwards and forwards along the stone. Rather like sawing squarely, this only comes with practice. It helps considerably when sharpening blades, if the oil-stone is held firmly in place. When you purchase one it will be supplied in a cardboard box. Take the trouble to make a shallow wooden box for it, preferably with a lid. The box can then by held in a vice while it is being used. After use, wipe away any dirty oil from the surface as this will contain tiny particles of steel which could clog the stone.

To keep a stone in good condition the surface must wear evenly, so avoid working only in one area when using the guide. Once a depression is formed in any part of the stone its performance will be impaired, the only remedy then would be to rub the surfaces of two stones together to even out the level.

If you are to keep blades in good working order, then you will make good use of your oil-stone. Sooner or later it will be necessary to renew the original grinding angle to a blade and this is where the coarse side of the stone comes into use.

Turn the stone in the box and apply oil to the surface as before, then use the guide with blade set in the correct position for grinding. It will take far longer to cut back the grinding angle, so you must patiently work over the stone for a much longer period.

A power-grinding machine will do this job far more quickly and you may decide to add a small grinding unit to your workshop in due course. Take car when using it as accidents can happen.

The grinder should have a spark guard fitted, if not wear some form of eye protection. Never let the blade get too hot through friction. Cool it in water each time you remove it from the grinding wheel. At all costs prevent the edge of the steel turning black due to burning as this will ruin its temper.

Surform plane

This is one of a range of surform tools, popular for removing roughness from wood. It is essentially a trimming tool rather than a smoothing tool and will not provide the very fine cut of a conventional plane. Surform tools often encourage beginners to work with other carpentry tools.

Replaceable blade plane

Inserting a new blade whenever required might appear easier than using a oil-stone. If you can, try to use one before committing yourself.

Electric planers

Compact planer units are now available for home use complete with a shavings collection bag. It is a power tool which you might like to add to your kit if you find sufficient need for it.

Chisels

Any chisel will be effortless and safer to use if it is razor sharp. Supplied lacquered when new, it requires honing in the same way as a plane blade to provide a cutting edge. Go for bevel-edged chisels with plastic handles. These can be struck with the side of a hammer head and do not require a mallet as the old wood-handle chisels do. In time you may build up a range of different size chisels, but the three likely to be of most use are a 6mm/$\frac{1}{4}$in, 12mm/$\frac{1}{2}$in and 25mm/1in.

Trimming knife

A multi-purpose cutting knife will complete your range of cutting tools. The standard blade is invaluable for scoring through the surface veneer of pre-finished boards before sawing them to size. Do this on all faces and follow up with a fine saw and this will prevent the grain tearing.

A whole variety of blades are available for use with a trimming knife for cutting other materials.

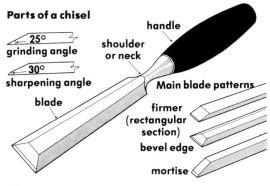

Parts of a chisel

25° grinding angle

30° sharpening angle

handle

shoulder or neck

blade

Main blade patterns

firmer (rectangular section)

bevel edge

mortise

Squares and Measures

Tape measure

Accuracy in carpentry is important and you will have to learn to measure correctly from the start. It is unfortunate that we are saddled with a mixture of metric and the old imperial dimensions in our daily lives and are likely to be so for some considerable time ahead. It is for this reason that a combined metric-imperial tape measure is useful and a 3m/10ft size is the one to buy. A good extending steel tape will last a long time if it is looked after, so make sure that it is never left in an extended position where it can be trodden on.

Tri square

The right angle plays an important part in most carpentry construction and a tri square has a role to play in checking this. A useful size is a 23cm/9in although larger and smaller sizes are available.

Combination square

This useful d.i.y tool incorporates several tools in one. The stock slides along a 305mm/12in rule to form a perfect right angle and a protractor forms angles ranging from 35° to 90°. It also has a spirit level vial and a screw gauge for wood screws No 4–12 built into the design.

Spirit level

There are several ways of finding a perfectly accurate level which is certainly necessary when it

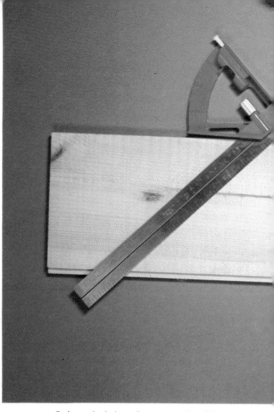

comes to fixing shelving for example. The longer the level the more accurate it will be, and it is certainly worth purchasing one with two vials, one for the horizontal and one for checking plumb vertical. You can check the accuracy of a level if in doubt.

Simply reverse the level to see if the bubble rests in the same place. Remember that the level of water will always be accurate and you can use this method by part filling a clear tray or clear plastic tube held in a U shape.

Plumb bob

This is a simple inexpensive tool to buy but probably one of the most useful in a tool kit. You

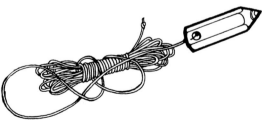

could make your own but it should have a perfectly balanced end weight to reduce the natural tendency for it to swing when suspended. With a plumb line you can check a true horizontal using a tri square set against it.

Hammers and Nails

A hammer is one of the first tools to be acquired for the household tool box and there are several different types to choose from. For the woodworker there are only two that really matter.

The claw hammer is the most useful as it will also extract nails from wood as well as driving them in. Available in various weights from 455–680g/16–24oz, the right one for you will depend largely on the strength of your wrist. Try the range for balance before making your choice and remember that a hammer is used by holding the handle at a point furthest away from the head.

Both steel and wooden shafts are used for claw hammers, but the steel shaft is slightly stronger. A point to remember when using the claw, is to put a small block of wood under the head if you are extracting long nails. This will provide extra leverage and also protect the surface of the timber beneath.

The Warrington or cross pein hammer has a flat wedge-shape pein instead of a claw and comes in a lighter range of weights from 170–455g/6–16oz. As the pein is used primarily for starting smaller nails and pins, it is worth having one of the lighter Warrington hammers for use on light-weight nails and pins which would be more difficult to drive with the heavier claw hammer.

There is another type of hammer which is useful to have about the home and this is the heavy club hammer. It is a short stubby hammer which weighs about 1360g/3lb and is held close to the head.

Although a club hammer would only be used on really heavy constructional jobs where timber is concerned, it is nevertheless a very useful tool for other building jobs involving masonry work where the conventional carpenter's hammer would be completely inadequate. Club hammers have wooden shafts and are difficult to use one handed if held at the end of the shaft.

There are two important safety points to observe where hammers are concerned. The first is to see that the striking head is kept clean and free of grease, to prevent it slipping during use. The second is never to work with a hammer head which is loose. At the first signs of looseness, check whether the wedges need replacing or whether a new shaft is required.

Using nails is the quickest and easiest method of joining wood together and this is often done with the addition of woodworking adhesive to give extra strength to the joint. There is a wide range of nails available and it is important to use the right nail for the job. These are the most common nails that you are likely to use:

Round wire nails
Used where strength is more important than appearance. Their large round heads help to pull the two sections of timber closely together. Sizes 20–150mm/¾in–6in.

Oval wire nails
Suitable for joinery where appearance dictates that they are driven below the surface and covered. Sizes 12–150mm/½in–6in.

Round or lost head nail
Another nail for driving below the surface. Sizes 12–150mm/½in–6in.

Cut clasp nail
This is a tapered square-cut nail with a head which is ideal for gripping wood and plugged masonry. Sizes 25–150mm/1in–6in.

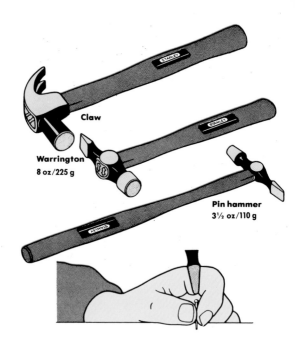

Claw

Warrington
8 oz/225 g

Pin hammer
3½ oz/110 g

Cut floor brads
Similar to a cut clasp nail but with a L-shaped head for fixing down floorboards. Size 12–150mm/$\frac{1}{2}$in–6in.

Panel pins
A small version of a lost head nail for light-weight work and fixing mouldings. Size 12–50mm/$\frac{1}{2}$in–2in.

Veneer pins
A small slender form of panel pin.

Hardboard nails
A panel pin with diamond shape head. Size 9–38mm/$\frac{3}{8}$in–1$\frac{1}{2}$in.

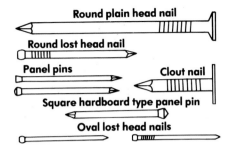

Round plain head nail

Round lost head nail

Panel pins

Clout nail

Square hardboard type panel pin

Oval lost head nails

Clout nails

A galvanized nail with a large round head for outside work – suitable for fixing down roofing felt. Non rusting. Sizes 12–50mm/$\frac{1}{2}$in–2in.

Masonry nails

A round nail of toughened steel, similar in appearance to a lost head nail. Can be hammered into brickwork and masonry. Sizes 20–100mm/$\frac{3}{4}$in–4in.

Tacks

These are square in section with flat heads and sharp points for fixing carpets. Sizes 20–32mm/$\frac{3}{4}$in–1$\frac{1}{4}$in.

Sprigs

Similar to tacks without heads. Used for holding in glass before applying putty. Sizes 12–20mm/$\frac{1}{2}$in–$\frac{3}{4}$in.

Upholstery nails

These are dome head nails used decoratively on upholstery. Available in various finishes such as chrome or brass.

Staples

Used for holding wire in place. They are U-shaped with two points and have an insulated lining when used for fixing electric cable.

It is useful to build up a small stock of the most common nails, keeping them in separate sizes.

Many suppliers stock only the blister packs which are an extremely expensive way to purchase nails. Shop around and try to find a retailer who sells them loose by weight, in this way you will get a lot more for your money and build your stock.

Considerable strength can be achieved when nails are used for structural jointing. One way to do this, when two pieces of wood are to be securely held together is to clench nail them. To do this, drive two nails through the wood in close proximity, one from each side so that the nails pass through both pieces from opposite directions. Allow about 25mm/1in of each nail to project through the back surface, then hammer them over and into the wood. If you angle a nail into timber it

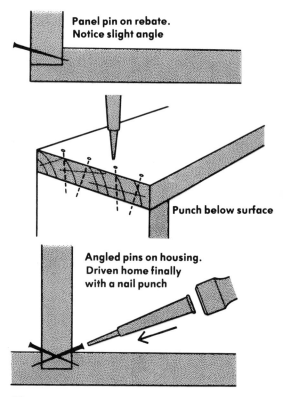

**Panel pin on rebate.
Notice slight angle**

Punch below surface

**Angled pins on housing.
Driven home finally
with a nail punch**

will hold more securely than if you drive it at right angles to the surface.

Where nails are used for structural assembly work in lofts for example, they are left exposed to view. On the other hand when they are used to assemble decorative work, they are usually hidden from sight on completion of the work. This does not present a problem where the surface is to be faced or painted, as they can be driven below the surface before the finishing work is carried out. One method of secret nailing can be employed on natural timber or even some veneered boards. Lift a sliver of the wood with a narrow chisel so that it remains attached at one end. Drive the nail into the cavity and glue the sliver back into place, lightly sanding down when the adhesive is dry.

You will certainly require a nail punch to drive nails below the surface and remember that if you are filling over steel nails with a water-based filler, rust could come through later. Where this could cause a problem, use galvanized nails. Drill pilot holes when nailing chipboard.

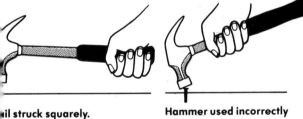

il struck squarely.
nd at bottom of shaft

Hammer used incorrectly

o upright

pack and pull to upright

or

waste wood to protect job

Screws and Screwdrivers

Screws provide a more secure form of fixing than nails and they can be far more decoratively employed, depending on the type of screw being used. There is a far greater range of finishes including steel, stainless steel, brass, chromium plated, sheradized and black japanned.

Screws are measured in two ways, the diameter of their shank and their overall size. The gauge of the shank ranges from No 4–14 and the length varies from 9–152mm/$\frac{3}{8}$in–6in.

There are several different types of screw which are identified by the design of their head.

Countersunk

This is the most common type with a tapering head which allows it to be driven flush with the surface or slightly below it.

Round head

This is a decorative screw which remains on the surface when holding fittings in place.

Raised head

Another decorative screw which is often used with a screw cup to hold thin material securely in place.

Dome head

This is used for fixing mirrors. The head is a countersunk slot screw which should be used with a rubber washer to hold the glass lightly in place –overtightening will cause cracking. A decorative domecap or cut glass boss screws into a threaded hole in the centre of the screw head.

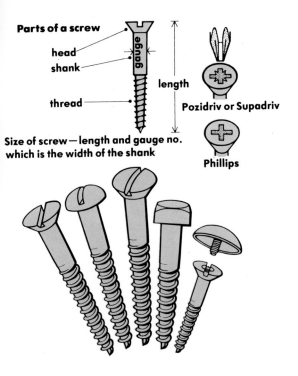

Parts of a screw

head

shank

gauge

length

thread

Size of screw — length and gauge no.
which is the width of the shank

Pozidriv or Supadriv

Phillips

Self tapping

This is most frequently used for sheet metal. It will
cut its own thread when driven into a small pilot
hole. Self tapping describes the type of thread: the
screws are available with raised, round or countersunk heads and the great majority are cross slotted.

Chipboard screw

This is a countersunk slot headed screw with a
large thread right up to the head to provide a
stronger grip than conventional screws.

Coach screws or bolts

A very stout screw which has a bolt type head for
strong fixings. Turned only by a spanner.

Take a look in any tool shop and you will see just
how many sizes of screwdriver there are in any one

particular range. This can be confusing especially if you are intending to buy one for the first time. The reason for this is easy to understand. The blade tip of a screwdriver must fit the head of a screw precisely or the screw head will be quickly damaged. This means that a number of different screwdrivers will be required if a wide range of screw sizes is used. This can be reduced to four initially if we consider the tip width of blade required for the most common gauges of screw:

Screw gauge	Tip width of screwdriver
No 4, No 6	5mm/$\frac{3}{16}$in
No 8	6mm/$\frac{1}{4}$in
No 10	8mm/$\frac{5}{16}$
No 12, No 14	9mm/$\frac{3}{8}$in

Then you must consider the length of the screwdriver blade. If for example you are working in a confined space, a short stubby one would be necessary whereas if the screw-head position was in a narrow opening at the back of a deep recess, a long reach blade would be essential.

In between these two extremities of length, there are all the standard sizes in any one range. So that if you work with a number of different screw sizes, then you will require several different screwdrivers. There would seem to be little alternative but to build up a kit, adding to it as necessity arises.

The Yankee screwdriver has proved popular over the years because of the advantages to be derived from using a choice of interchangeable blades. Coupled with its push action for speed, it provides several different screwdrivers in one. There are also various small push drill bits which can be used with it for boring starter holes for screws. The Yankee model comes in various sizes but the small handyman version is a useful tool to have in your kit.

Cross slot screw heads are often badly damaged

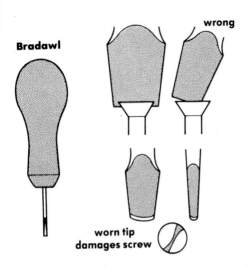

Bradawl

wrong

worn tip
damages screw

Parts of a screwdriver

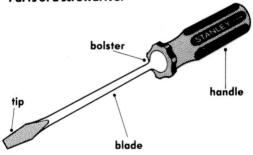

bolster

handle

tip

blade

Before a screw is inserted

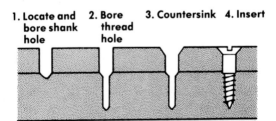

1. Locate and bore shank hole
2. Bore thread hole
3. Countersink
4. Insert

because the wrong screwdriver has been used with them. The most recent development in cross slot heads is the Supadriv screw which has now superseded its predecessor the Pozidriv screw. The Pozidriv screwdriver should be used with both but you will find that a far better grip is provided by the Supadriv head when turning, even when the blade is not completely square onto it.

The Phillips screwdriver should still be used with the old type Phillips cross slot screw head, most of which are found in electrical appliances.

The Yankee screwdriver will accommodate interchangeable bits for cross head screws, and reference to a catalogue will show several different

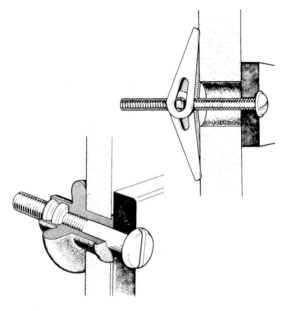

For fixing into a cavity wall, special fixings are available. Here are two of them. The spring toggle has wings which open after insertion through the hole and cannot be withdrawn and re-used. The Rawlnut can be withdrawn.

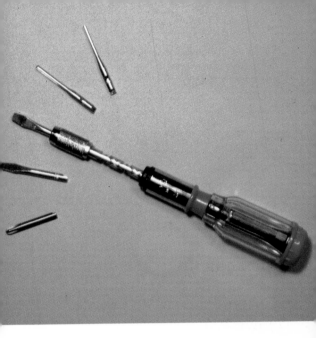

screwdrivers for use with this type of screw. They vary in length and point size.

Take the greatest care of a screwdriver blade. Resist the temptation to use it for any purpose which will damage it. A damaged blade will ruin the head of a perfectly good screw and render it useless should you want to loosen or tighten it. With care you can cut a new square edge to a blade but you will need a grind stone to do it.

There are simple rules to follow when screwing two pieces of wood together, particularly when using hardwoods. A clearance hole should be drilled through the first piece to allow the shank of the screw to pass freely. If countersinking is required, this can be done at the same time. Then a pilot hole should be made in the second piece of timber as a guide for the screw. This can be made with a twist drill, push drill or bradawl or there is a special bit called a screwmate which will drill all three sections at the same time.

The following guide will give a clearer idea of the dimensions required.

Screw gauge	Clearance hole
No 4	$3mm/\frac{1}{8}in$
No 6	$4mm/\frac{5}{32}in$
No 8	$5mm/\frac{3}{16}in$
No 10	$5mm/\frac{3}{16}in$
No 12	$6mm/\frac{1}{4}in$
No 14	$6mm/\frac{1}{4}in$

Pilot hole hardwood	Pilot hole softwood
$2mm/\frac{5}{64}in$	bradawl
$2mm/\frac{5}{64}in$	bradawl
$3mm/\frac{1}{8}in$	$2mm/\frac{5}{64}in$
$3mm/\frac{1}{8}in$	$2mm/\frac{5}{8}in$
$4mm/\frac{5}{32}in$	$3mm/\frac{1}{8}in$
$5mm/\frac{3}{16}in$	$4mm/\frac{5}{32}in$

End grain does not give a strong anchorage for screws but the addition of glue between the surfaces helps to increase the strength. Another method of re-inforcing a joint is to drill and insert a dowel across the grain a suitable distance from the end. Sufficiently long screws will then have to be used to reach through to the dowel.

Screw fixings into masonry or brickwork will be perfectly secure as long as the wall fixing plug is properly anchored. With a thick soft plaster this can mean drilling deeply into the solid wall behind it – the plaster is purely cosmetic and offers no grip to the plug at all.

The screw should then drive in positively and lock tight on the final turn without entailing a major struggle. If you meet slightly more resistance than you bargained for on the final turns, remove the screw and smear a little soap along the thread for lubrication. Brass- and chromium-plated screws are softer than steel and consequently do not take kindly to excessive stress.

Clamps

If you already possess a Workmate, then you will find that this remarkable piece of equipment provides you with a range of clamping facilities. The long jaws will grip objects with parallel and tapering sides and the slot-in pegs can be arranged to hold other shapes rigidly on top of the bench.

Similarly a portable or bench-mounted vice can be useful for clamping wood firmly in place, either for working purposes or small gluing operations. To minimize any damage to the workpiece when using a vice, it helps considerably if the jaws are lined with replaceable pieces of plywood. Take care at all times to avoid bruising the surface of the workpiece, especially if it is nearing its finishing stages. Small off-cuts which you have saved can often help here.

Where pressure is required over a large area, improvisation will often provide you with the type of pressure you require. This can be done by using the well-tried tourniquet method where joints are closed up by twisting a stout cord with a small piece of wood between the cord acting as a winder. This method of using a cord is often known as the Spanish windlass. It is expensive and flexible in its application.

Off-cuts are useful for forming wedges which can be used to apply pressure. A large frame or workpiece for example can be placed between two pieces of wood screwed securely in place on a workbench.

Sufficient space should be allowed along one side of the frame to insert a pair of folding wedges – these are two wedges pointing in opposite directions. Gently tap the wedges alternatively from either side and this will squeeze the workpiece against the fixed timber, locking the improvised clamp firmly together. If a frame is being glued in this way, you should see the surplus glue exuding from the joints as they close up.

This principle can be applied to many jobs; however it is always useful to have one or two extra clamps in your kit for immediate use.

G-clamps

Steel G-clamps are sized according to the jaw opening, the most common being 50–300mm/ 2in–12in. The threaded screw jaw is fitted with a swivel foot to adjust to sloping surfaces. It is perfectly suited to clamping timber to a work surface or for putting localized pressure to a glued area between two pieces of wood.

Edging clamp

This is a special version of a small G-clamp, used for holding edging and lippings securely in place. When the clamp is tightened onto the workpiece, a secondary screw can be tightened, closing another jaw at 90° to the main jaw.

Sash clamps

These are useful if you need to glue up large frames and are unable to use the improvised method described above. They are expensive and are only worth purchasing if you can make regular use of them.

Web clamp

By contrast this is a cheap method of applying pressure to large panels or frames using nylon webbing. The nylon webbing is passed around the

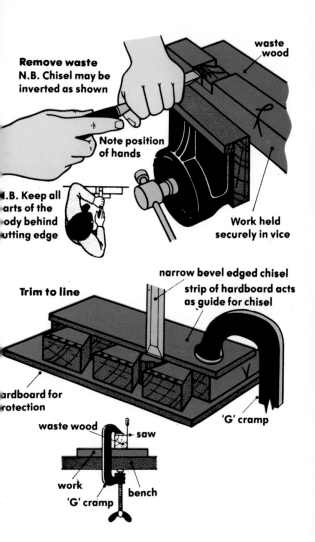

Remove waste
N.B. Chisel may be inverted as shown

waste wood

Note position of hands

N.B. Keep all parts of the body behind cutting edge

Work held securely in vice

Trim to line

narrow bevel edged chisel
strip of hardboard acts as guide for chisel

hardboard for protection

'G' cramp

waste wood — **saw**

work   **bench**

'G' cramp

outer edge of the workpiece and tightened through a steel clamp with a ratchet mechanism. This type of clamp has the advantage of being suitable around almost any shape of framework. The length of the nylon webbing is 3.5mm/12ft.

Making Joints

The more traditional carpentry joints such as dovetails call for considerable skill and are only likely to be tackled by the real woodworking enthusiast. There are however several other ways that joints can be made with natural timber.

Halving joints

This is probably one of the easiest ways of joining two pieces of wood for framework and consists of recesses being cut into both pieces, so that when they are brought together, all the surfaces are flush. Usually the joint is glued and screwed for additional strength.

The T joint and cross joint require the use of a chisel to remove the waste timber after the saw cuts have been made to the correct depth with a tenon saw. The T joint can be dovetail cut. The angle or corner halving joint consists of two sawn shoulders which may require a slight cleaning up with a chisel before assembly.

A mitre halving joint is another method of forming a frame corner. As the saw cuts are made at $45°$ angles, only half the amount of wood is removed from each piece compared to the L joint.

Housing joint

A popular joint for shelving where the end of the cross piece is let into the side of the upright. This joint is mostly made with timber of equal width and thickness. If the housing groove is taken through the full width of the side upright, the joint is known as a through housing, whereas if it does not reach the outer surface, the term stopped housing is used.

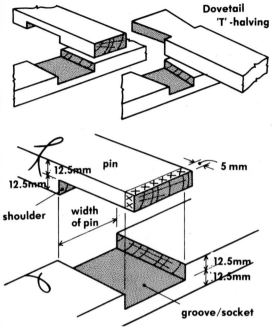

Dovetail 'T'-halving

12.5mm pin 5 mm

12.5mm

shoulder width of pin

12.5mm
12.5mm

groove/socket

All marking carried out from the face side or face edge

Dowel joint

Dowels can be cut from lengths of dowel rod and as a general rule they would be about four times the length of the diameter of the rod. A shallow groove should be made along the side of the dowel to allow surplus glue to escape and both ends should be slightly shamfered.

The secret of good dowel jointing is accuracy. Above all accuracy of measurement to see that the centre point marking on both surfaces are perfectly in line. Then the holes should be plumb vertical in each case, drilled to the exact diameter of the dowel and precisely the depth to allow the joint to close up tightly. All three requirements can be met with the aid of a dowel jig and there are several inexpensive jigs on the market to choose from.

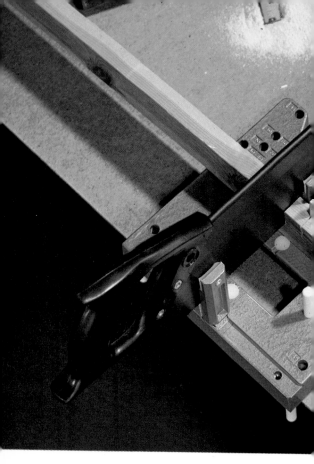

Mitre joint

The straight mitre is used mainly for picture frames and its strength relies mainly on adhesive with the additional use of pins.

To cut an accurate mitre, you will certainly need a mitre box or sawing jig to form a perfect 45° cut – a Jointmaster is an ideal tool for the job and will enable a number of other joints to be made efficiently.

The difficult part of the operation lies in joining the mitres squarely at all four corners. A Stanley

frame clamp can be used, which is another alternative to the Spanish windlass. There are four right angle jaws of polypropylene plastic to protect the corners of the frame, and 3.5m/12ft of terrylene cord which pulls tightly through a cleat to draw the corners together.

If a mitred corner is to be pinned, the frame will have to be held securely in a vice with adequate protection for the frame itself while the pin is inserted.

The mortice and tenon

The tenon should be cut cleanly with a tenon saw, remembering always to saw on the waste side of the line. Drill out the mortice working from both faces of the timber to ensure a series of clean holes within the marked lines. The cavity can then be cleaned out squarely with a sharp chisel.

The through tenon is the most commonly used joint. The tenon should be cut fractionally over length and the mortice should widen out slightly on the outer side. This will allow for thin wedges to be tapped into place to lock the joint. Assemble the two parts with a thin coating of glue on the contacting surfaces then clamp until it is thoroughly dry. The projecting tenon and wedges can be planed back flush to the surface.

A stub tenon is a neater version of the joint. The tenon stops short and does not appear on the outside. The joint is strengthened after assembly with dowels which can either be taken right through to be visible on both faces, or stop short once they have pierced the tenon. Other variations of this joint include the T bridal and angle bridal.

Joining man-made boards

So far we have only considered joining natural timber together. When it comes to man-made boards, the conventional methods of jointing cannot be used and other techniques must be employed.

For pre-finished boards, assembly joints are available to provide maximum strength and these are frequently used in kitchen cabinets and other types of knock-down furniture. The joint is in two parts which are screwed separately to the face of each board in perfect alignment to form a solid joint when they are bolted together. Another method of fixing can be achieved with the one part rigid joint. These are made from thermoplastic and should be used with chipboard screws.

Both types of joint are clearly visible when fitted and are best employed on unit constructions where they can be hidden away behind closed doors. A less obtrusive method of fixing can be provided with countersunk screws set into chipboard plugs. These plugs are first glued into the chipboard in the appropriate fixing positions to provide additional holding strength for the screw. The screw heads can then be flush covered with plastic caps, or set in raised plastic socket rings with snap-on covers, leaving them slightly proud of the surface.

Where a construction is made from chipboard, plywood or blockboard to be painted or covered with a facing material such as laminated plastic, screw or nails can be used with adhesive to form the joint. This will provide a concealed fixing and we shall consider the method of applying laminates later on, but first a word about adhesives and their use in carpentry joints.

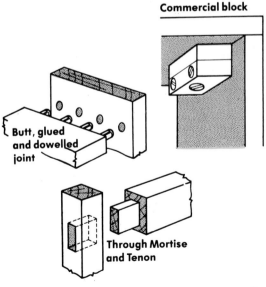

Commercial block

Butt, glued and dowelled joint

Through Mortise and Tenon

ADHESIVES

Animal glues have been used by craftsmen for centuries and are still used for restoring and repairing some antiques today. Modern technology has introduced a new range of convenience adhesives and there are three different types which are most frequently used for woodwork.

PVA or woodworking adhesive

This is the most common type used for carpentry. It is suitable for all natural timbers and man-made boards which are to be confined to dry environments. It will set within one hour in reasonable room conditions and needs to dry under pressure.

Water and heat resistant adhesive

This is usually supplied in powder form and mixed with water. As a gap-filling adhesive it is spread evenly between surfaces and clamped under pressure until dry. Setting time can take up to 6 hours depending on the room temperature. Once dry it is completely waterproof and so used in boat building and garden furniture making.

Impact or contact adhesive – petroleum based

A highly flammable material which must be used in well ventilated conditions. A non-flammable version is available which provides an instant bond without the need for sustained pressure. Both surfaces should be evenly coated using a spreader, then when touch dry, they should be carefully aligned and brought together. Re-alignment is extremely difficult after contact has been made.

To give the final bond, go over the surface with a block of wood and hammer, tapping every few inches. This adhesive is also available in a non-drip version which is very useful for vertical and overhead surfaces where the free flow material tends to run off the spreader.

Sanding and Finishing

However well a piece of carpentry has been made, the end product can certainly be enhanced or ruined by the final stages of finishing and pre-finishing. Pre-finishing consists of preparing the surface thoroughly with a scraper or abrasives.

Cabinet scraper

Before we consider the various abrasive papers and sanding tools available for use on timber surfaces, a word first about a very useful tool, a cabinet scraper.

There are scrapers available with replaceable blades but undoubtedly the most economic version is a simple rectangle of saw steel, which can be repeatedly sharpened by running a file squarely along each edge. The file forms a small steel burr along either side of each edge, providing eight cutting blades. When the scraper is pulled firmly back across the timber at a slight angle, all loose fibres and other roughness is removed as a fine dust. You will know when the cutting edge begins to lose its sharpness. The scraper will remove old polish, varnish and paint just as effectively and can save the outlay on more sheets of abrasive paper than are necessary.

Abrasive papers

The term sandpaper or glasspaper is used to cover a whole range of different types of abrasive paper. Crushed glass is used on the cheapest form,

whereas garnet and aluminium oxide are longer lasting and more expensive.

For woodwork abrasive paper should be used dry, the wet and dry version is commonly used to rub down old paintwork. Always use abrasive paper wrapped firmly around a cork block.

WOOD FINISHES

Most natural timber has an inherent beauty which is worth preserving and enhancing, so that every means should be employed to make the most of the wood which you have used. On the other hand, should you have worked with a material which does not posses these qualities, you may decide to paint it so as to hide not only the defects in the timber itself, but also any blemishes in the actual construction. Remember to apply a coat of shellac knotting to any resinous areas or knots and to prime with metal primer any exposed steel screw or nail heads before using a water-based filler. Having taken this precaution, you can then proceed with the undercoating and finishing paint in the normal way.

Stains and dyes

Should you decide to retain the natural grain of the timber, you may want to adjust the colour with a stain before applying the final finish to it. Before

72

using a stain it may be necessary to apply a grain filler to any cavities or unevenness in the surface. Care should be taken to see that the grain filler is as close a match in colour to the stain as possible. It is usually open grained hard woods like oak which require the use of grain filler.

Oil stain colours are applied with a clean dry cloth and there are several shades of stain to choose from both in the oil stain and water-based dye ranges.

If you use a water-based wood dye it may be inclined to raise the grain a little. If it does, let it dry thoroughly then lightly rub down the surface with a very fine grade of abrasive paper.

Polyurethane

This can be applied over the stain in a clear gloss or matt finish. For really hardwearing surfaces build up two or three brush applied coats.

French polish

Before the development of modern polyurethane varnish and other synthetic finishes, French polish was traditionally used as a furniture finish. Although it provided a high sheen, it was not resistant to heat or water and was liable to scratch easily. It is still used today although considerable patience and a certain amount of skill is needed to achieve a high-quality finish.

French polish consists of shellac and methylated spirit which is obtainable ready mixed for use. It is

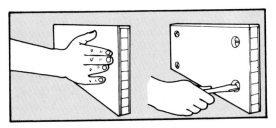

applied in a series of strokes worked in a loop pattern, using a rubber made up from soft rag, wrapped around a wad of cotton wool in a pear-shape fashion. As the spirit evaporates the rubber becomes more difficult to move and this can be remedied by applying a few drops of linseed oil on the rubber for lubrication – too much oil will cause the surface to smear. The final stage is the most crucial. The polish in the rubber should be thinned with methylated spirit and rubbed out nearly dry on a spare piece of wood before being used again on the surface to provide the final sheen which should be glass like and free of smears.

POWER SANDERS

Let us return to the important stage of pre-finishing your woodwork and consider the advantages to be gained by using a power sander. There are four different types of power sander available but only one of them is really suitable to provide the degree of pre-finish to a surface comparable to the standard which can be achieved by hand. So let us consider that one first.

Orbital sander

This is the finishing sander with a vibrating action. Sanding sheets fit over a rectangular base which are easily detached when changing the grade of sheet. Recent models incorporate a dust collection bag which is useful when working inside the house. Although the orbital sander creates less dust than the other power sanders, it is still a great advantage to be able to collect at source.

Belt sander

This is also fitted with a dust collection bag and is essentially used for coarse sanding such as taking the top surface from old floorboards.

Drum sander

This is a drill attachment consisting of a sanding belt fitted around a drum of soft foam. Used with the direction of the grain it will remove old paintwork effectively but should preferably be used outside.

The sanding disc

This is another drill attachment and is certainly not to be recommended as a wood finishing sander. The circular turn of the abrasive disc can badly score the surface of timber.

Teak oil

Where a matt natural finish is required teak oil can be rubbed into the grain. It is quick drying with a pleasant smell and two or three applications can be made in a short period of time. Pre-finished veneered boards look particularly attractive when finished in this way but surfaces which are subject to hard wear and frequent wiping down should not be treated with teak oil.

LAMINATED PLASTIC

As a complete contrast to delicate wood finishes, the application of a decorative laminate such as Formica provides the ultimate hardwearing surface for covering man-made boards, such as chipboard.

Master the three techniques of cutting, bonding and trimming and you will have the confidence to tackle any job in the home involving the use of this material. Small pieces can be cut using a veneer saw held at a shallow angle with the decorative face uppermost. When you progress to cutting larger sizes, there is no better place to do this than on the floor. Lay a full sheet decorative face upwards and mark the cutting lines in pencil allowing a little extra width for trimming later.

Protect the floor with an off-cut of hardboard stretching under the cutting line, then with a straight edge placed on the laminate firmly against the line, score the surface with a laminate scribing tool or trimming knife fitted with a laminate cutting blade. Continue scoring against the straight edge until you get through to the back, or when only half way through lift the laminate upwards against the straight edge to give a clean snap along the line.

The most practical method of bonding a plastic laminate to the surface, is with an impact or contact adhesive. As this is a petroleum-based material with a high evaporation rate, plenty of ventilation is required when using it. It is wise to refrain from using it in really hot weather if large areas are to be covered.

The adhesive should be spread evenly on the back of the laminate and the surface of the core board. Large areas can be covered with adhesive fairly rapidly using the comb spreader supplied with the tin.

Accurate alignment of the laminate with the core board is imperative once the adhesive has become touch dry. It should be put into position allowing a slight overhang for trimming and then bonded by tapping the entire surface with a block of wood and hammer.

Wherever a surface is to be subjected to excessive water, a waterproof gap-filling adhesive should be used and allowed to dry under pressure. Care is needed if the trimming is to be carried out successfully. Use a sharp block plane with the mouth closed down to trim back most of the overhang, then finish off with a file or cabinet scraper. Always file towards the decorative face of the laminate and never away from it for fear of chipping away the top surface.

Edging strips can be cut from larger pieces and these shoud be applied before fixing the top surface. On a porous core board it is wise to prime the edge with a thin application of contact adhesive and allow it to dry before sticking down the edging strip with a second coat of the adhesive. If you use a waterproof adhesive for edging, it can be held in position with strips of adhesive tape to provide the necessary pressure while drying. A laminate surface can also be edged with a hardwood lipping, stuck in a similar manner using tape. This type of lipping will provide a greater degree of protection against damage. Should bruising occur to the hardwood, it can be skimmed back with a plane to form a clean edge to the worktop.

Finally an iron edging can be purchased in roll form to stick to sawn edges of boards. Here again it is worthwhile priming the edge of the board first with adhesive to kill the suction. Use a warm iron and some protective brown paper to apply the edging strip – the iron will soften the self-adhesive back of the strip and enable it to stick firmly into place. Do not have the iron too hot as this could lead to scorching the veneer. Once the adhesive has dried, any slight overhang can be rubbed down with a fine abrasive paper.

Here the author has designed and built a wall unit for a small kitchen which has a sloping ceiling. The carcase was first assembled from pieces of 18mm/¾in chipboard screwed to a 9mm/⅜in plywood backing. The unit was then fixed to the wall and the fixing screws covered with ceramic tiles to match the surrounding wall area. In this instance front edging strips of white Formica were applied after all other exposed chipboard surfaces had been covered and trimmed. A fitment constructed in this way is completely maintenance free and only needs wiping down from time to time with a damp cloth to remove dust.

Repairs in the Home

There is no better way to experiment with laminates than on the skirting boards at home. This can have a practical advantage if you plan to have fitted carpet in a room as repainting skirtings with fitted carpets can present a major problem. Laminates cannot be applied directly onto painted surfaces but this problem can be overcome by nailing thin ply over existing paintwork. If new skirtings are to be fitted, then apply and trim the top edge with laminate before fixing them in place. The front face will then conceal the fixing screws.

Shop around and you may find some suitable off-cuts of laminate to use on your skirtings. If you select a timber pattern with the grain running vertically up the skirting, you will find that the joins are barely visible. It is more difficult to match a grain running the length of the skirting.

Replacing a floorboard

If you live in an older dwelling make a point of checking the condition of the floorboards. Suspended timber floors were used in domestic dwellings until solid concrete started to replace the traditional timber construction.

If you find that the condition of a timber floor is poor throughout, then it is probably wise to consider replacing all the existing boards with flooring-grade chipboard. Alternatively, it may be only one particular board which is in poor condition and requires replacing. First check the

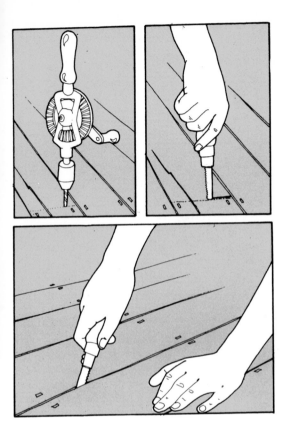

type of boards which have been used. These will either be square edge or tongued and grooved. If you can slide a thin blade between them they will be square edged. The blade will not get very far if they are T and G boards and a small pilot hole will have to be drilled to enable a pad saw blade to cut along the tongues. Next cut one end of the damaged board as close to the joist as possible using the same method of pilot hole and pad saw. The nail heads will give you a guide as to the joist position.

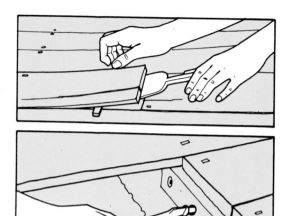

Before sawing the board switch off the main power supply as a safeguard against loose electric cables lying underneath. Slide a wide cold chisel or brick bolster into the gap and level upwards, once the board end begins to lift, slide a piece of wood underneath and work along the entire length of the board. When the board is clear you will then see if any pipes or cables are lurking below.

Get a new board cut to the size of the one which you are replacing – if the supplier cannot provide the exact thickness then it is better to get one slightly oversize and plane it back when it is in position. See that the nail heads are driven below the surface before you use your plane. Your original saw cut will have been along the side of the joist so you will need to screw a stout batten to it to provide a fixing for the new board. Rather than use nails here, fix the board at this end with a couple of countersunk screws.

Stair treads

A creaking staircase can be annoying and can often be put right if you have ready access to the space under the stairs. It may be just one or two treads which are at fault due to movement. First check whether the wedges are loose – if they are apply adhesive and tap them tightly back into position.

A carriage block may have come loose and this will have to be glued and nailed back into place. Alternatively screw a metal angle bracket in its place. If it is not possible to get at these areas conveniently, look at the tread itself, it might be possible to insert screws from the top surface to overcome the problem.

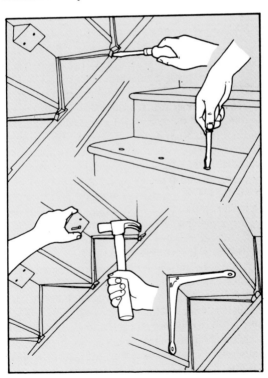

Door rattle

This is usually due to a gap between the door and the door stop moulding on the frame. It can be rectified easily by moving the keep plate back to compensate – simply unscrew it and replace it in the correct position. You may have to trim some wood away to allow the lock catch to pass into the frame.

Flush panelling a door

Although traditional panelled doors can be most attractive, particularly in old Victorian houses, nevertheless flush doors are often preferred for the ease with which they can be painted.

Hardboard or thin plywood can be used to face both sides of the door but first the levels of the panels will have to be made up by fixing infill pieces of the correct thickness. Then there is the tricky job of applying hardwood lipping to each long edge to protect the thin edges of the facing panels. To do this the lock, handles and hinges will have to be temporarily removed. Then approximately 10mm/⅜in will have to be sawn from each long edge of the door – which is the normal thickness of the hardwood lipping. This lipping can be glued and pinned into place. Finally cut new hinge recesses and the lock aperture to match the originals. Once the fittings are back in place the door can be re-hung – remember that it will be slightly thicker and heavier than before.

Trimming doors

A new carpet can present a problem, especially if you have chosen one with a deeper pile than its predecessor. This may mean trimming the underside of the door, so you will have to take it down from its frame. Before you attempt to unscrew the hinges see that the screw slots are free of paint. If a screw is difficult to turn, try tightening it first. Failing this, if it remains stubborn, tap the

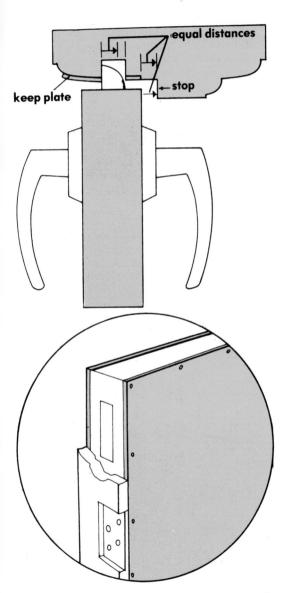

equal distances

keep plate

stop

screwdriver having first placed the blade tip in contact with the right hand side of the screw slot. Once there is the slightest movement in an anti-clockwise direction, centre the blade and continue unscrewing.

Mark a trimming line along the bottom of the door and if it is less than 6mm/$\frac{1}{4}$in, use a sharp plane working in from each end. Anything wider should be sawn off and then skimmed with a plane.

The other way to raise a door is to fit rising-butt hinges. The door will still have to be taken down from its frame and the hinges completely removed, but it will not be necessary to trim anything from the bottom.

The rising-butt hinge comes in two separate halves. The socket plate fits to the door and the spindle plate to the door frame. If a screw hole becomes oversize, drill it out and insert a wall plug, or glue in a piece of wood dowel before making another pilot hole for the screw.

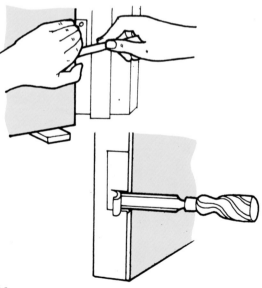

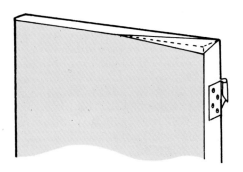

Use a plane to shamfer the top of the door from the hinge edge, tapering back towards the centre. Take off a little at a time so that it just clears the frame. With rising butts fitted, the door can be lifted away easily.

You will have to shamfer the closing top back edge of the door. Take off sufficient to allow it to clear the frame as the butt rises.

Repairs to furniture legs

The strain exerted by a fitted castor can cause a furniture leg to split. The remedy is to remove the castor and castor housing, wedge open the split carefully and squirt adhesive into it. Clamp the joint together and drive back the castor housing while the clamps are still in place. Push back the castor when the joint is dry.

Chairs wobble because legs are of unequal length. Level the chair by placing packing pieces under the shorter legs. The problem can then be remedied in one of two ways. Either trim back the longer legs to the thickness of the packing or glue and pin shaped pieces from matching timber to the shorter legs to make up the level.

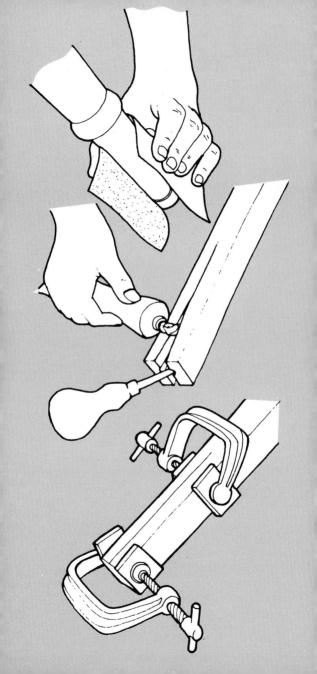